Table Of Contents

Chapter 1: Understanding Artificial Intelligence

What is AI?

Artificial Intelligence, commonly referred to as AI, encompasses a broad field of computer science dedicated to creating machines and systems capable of performing tasks that typically require human intelligence. This includes activities such as understanding natural language, recognizing patterns, solving problems, and making decisions. AI systems can analyze vast amounts of data quickly and accurately, enabling them to learn from experiences and improve over time. As technology has advanced, AI has become more integrated into our daily lives, influencing various sectors, from healthcare to education and beyond.

At its core, AI can be categorized into two main types: narrow AI and general AI. **Narrow AI** is designed to perform specific tasks, such as virtual assistants like Siri or Alexa, which can respond to voice commands or manage smart home devices. In contrast, **general AI** remains largely theoretical and refers to machines that possess the ability to understand and reason across a wide range of subjects, similar to human intelligence. Currently, most AI applications we encounter are examples of narrow AI, which are tailored to meet particular needs and enhance our daily activities.

In the realm of personal productivity, AI tools are revolutionizing time management. Applications like calendar schedulers and task automation software help users streamline their daily routines by organizing appointments, setting reminders, and even prioritizing tasks based on deadlines. By integrating AI into time management practices, individuals can maximize their efficiency, allowing them to focus on more critical responsibilities and personal interests.

AI also plays a significant role in personal finance, providing users with tools for budgeting, investment assistance, and financial planning. Smart budgeting apps can analyze spending habits and suggest areas for improvement, while AI-driven investment platforms offer personalized strategies based on individual goals and risk tolerance. By leveraging AI in personal finance, users can make informed decisions that lead to better financial health and long-term wealth accumulation.

AI also influences learning and creativity significantly. AI-driven educational tools can provide customized learning experiences that adjust to each student's pace and style, improving understanding and retention. In the realm of creativity, AI tools help produce art, compose music, and support writing, enabling creators to venture into new possibilities while boosting their productivity. As AI

2

progresses, its use in fields such as travel planning and shopping is streamlining decision-making, offering personalized recommendations and making daily tasks easier to handle.

The History of AI

The history of artificial intelligence (AI) begins in the mid-20th century, emerging from a blend of computer science, cognitive psychology, and linguistics. The term "artificial intelligence" was first coined in 1956 at a conference at Dartmouth College, where visionaries like John McCarthy and Marvin Minsky gathered to explore the potential of machines to simulate human intelligence. Early AI research focused on problem-solving and symbolic methods, laying the groundwork for future developments. Initial successes included programs that could play games like chess and solve mathematical problems, demonstrating that computers could perform tasks that required human-like reasoning.

As the decades progressed, AI research experienced periods of both optimism and disillusionment, often referred to as "AI winters." During these times, funding and interest waned due to unmet expectations and the challenges of creating truly intelligent systems. However, advancements in hardware, algorithms, and data availability eventually reignited interest in AI during the 1990s and 2000s. The introduction of machine learning, particularly deep learning, revolutionized the field by enabling computers to learn from vast amounts of data and improve their performance over time. This shift marked a significant turning point, positioning AI as a transformative technology across various sectors.

The 21st century has witnessed an exponential growth in AI applications, driven largely by improvements in computational power and the availability of big data. Today, AI is integrated into numerous aspects of daily life, enhancing productivity and efficiency in personal and professional settings. For instance, AI tools assist in time management by offering scheduling suggestions, automating reminders, and prioritizing tasks. These capabilities enable individuals to streamline their daily routines, making it easier to balance work, personal commitments, and leisure activities.

In the realm of personal finance, AI has emerged as a vital resource for budgeting and investment assistance. Financial apps powered by AI analyze spending habits, recommend personalized savings plans, and even provide insights into investment opportunities tailored to individual risk profiles. This democratization of financial advice empowers users to make informed decisions and optimize their financial well-being, showcasing how AI can directly enhance everyday life.

Furthermore, AI's creative applications are reshaping how we interact with art, music, and content creation. From AI-generated paintings to music composition and even writing assistance, these tools are democratizing creativity, allowing individuals to explore new forms of expression. Additionally, AI simplifies travel planning by offering personalized itineraries and booking recommendations based on user preferences. In shopping, AI analyzes consumer behavior to deliver tailored recommendations and exclusive deals, transforming the shopping experience. As AI continues to evolve, its integration into daily life will likely deepen, making it an indispensable companion in our modern world.

How AI Works

Artificial Intelligence (AI) operates through a combination of algorithms, data, and computational power. At its core, AI mimics human cognitive functions such as learning, reasoning, and problem-solving. These systems analyze vast amounts of data to identify patterns and make predictions. For everyday applications, this means that AI can help automate tasks, provide personalized recommendations, and enhance decision-making processes in various aspects of life.

Machine learning is a significant subset of AI that allows computers to learn from data without being explicitly programmed. Algorithms are designed to improve their performance as they process more information. For example, in personal finance, AI tools can analyze spending habits and suggest budgeting strategies tailored to individual needs. Similarly, in time management, AI applications can learn from user behavior to recommend optimal schedules and task prioritization, ultimately leading to increased productivity.

Natural language processing (NLP) is another crucial component of AI that enables machines to understand and interpret human language. This capability is particularly useful in educational tools, where AI can facilitate personalized learning experiences. For instance, AI-driven platforms can assess a student's understanding of a subject and adjust the curriculum accordingly, making learning more efficient and engaging. In creative fields, NLP allows for the generation of written content, transforming how we approach writing and content creation.

In the realm of travel planning, AI simplifies the process by analyzing preferences and past behaviors to curate personalized itineraries. Travel applications can suggest destinations, accommodations, and activities based on user input and historical data. This capability not only saves time but also enhances the travel experience by ensuring that itineraries align with individual interests and budgets. AI's ability to process large datasets quickly allows for real-time updates and recommendations, making travel planning more accessible and enjoyable.

Shopping has also been revolutionized by AI, as algorithms analyze consumer behavior to provide tailored recommendations. E-commerce platforms utilize AI to suggest products based on previous purchases and browsing history, resulting in a more personalized shopping experience. Additionally, AI can help users find the best deals and discounts, maximizing their budgets. As AI continues to evolve, its applications in daily life become increasingly integral, making tasks simpler and more efficient across various domains.

Chapter 2: How to Use AI in Daily Life

AI Assistants and Personal Helpers

AI assistants and personal helpers have become integral to our daily routines, offering a range of functionalities designed to simplify tasks and enhance productivity. These digital companions, powered by artificial intelligence, can manage schedules, set reminders, and even automate mundane chores. As technology continues to advance, these tools are increasingly capable of understanding natural language, making interactions more intuitive and human-like. For anyone looking to streamline their day-to-day activities, leveraging AI assistants can be a game-changing experience.

One of the most significant advantages of AI assistants is their ability to manage time effectively. Tools like virtual calendars and task management applications can help users prioritize tasks, set deadlines, and allocate time efficiently. For instance, AI can analyze your habits and suggest optimal times for meetings or focus periods, ensuring that your day is structured for maximum productivity. By taking over the logistics of scheduling, these assistants free up mental space, allowing individuals to concentrate on more important tasks or creative endeavors.

In the realm of personal finance, AI assistants are proving invaluable. With budgeting and investment assistance, users can gain insights into their spending habits through AI-driven analysis. Many financial apps now utilize AI to track expenses, suggest savings strategies, and even recommend investment opportunities based on personal goals and risk tolerance. This level of tailored financial guidance helps individuals make informed decisions, ultimately leading to better financial health and a deeper understanding of their economic landscape.

AI is also transforming the way we learn and access educational resources. Personalized learning platforms powered by AI can adapt to individual learning styles and paces, providing customized content that is more effective than traditional methods. These tools can recommend courses, track progress, and even offer tutoring in various subjects, making education more accessible and tailored to personal needs. For students and lifelong learners alike, AI-driven educational resources can enhance the learning experience, making it more engaging and productive.

Finally, AI's creative applications are expanding rapidly, influencing art, music, and content creation. AI tools can assist in generating original artwork, composing music, or even drafting written content, providing users with a collaborative partner in their creative endeavors. These services empower individuals to explore their artistic potential, breaking down barriers to creativity by offering suggestions, inspiration, and even technical assistance. As AI continues to evolve, its role in personal expression and creativity will likely grow, making it an essential resource for anyone looking to innovate in their artistic pursuits.

Smart Home Devices

Smart home devices are revolutionizing the way we interact with our living spaces, enhancing convenience, security, and energy efficiency. These devices utilize artificial intelligence to learn user preferences and automate routine tasks. From smart speakers that respond to voice commands to intelligent thermostats that adjust the temperature based on occupancy, these technologies simplify daily life. By integrating with other devices and systems, smart home technology creates an interconnected environment that allows users to manage their homes from a centralized interface, often accessible via smartphones or tablets.

One of the primary benefits of smart home devices is their ability to streamline time management. For instance, smart assistants like Amazon's Alexa or Google Assistant can help users set reminders, manage schedules, and even control other connected devices with simple voice commands. This capability not only saves time but also reduces the cognitive load of remembering tasks and appointments. When combined with smart lighting and automated appliances, users can create routines that align with their daily schedules, such as having lights turn on at sunrise or coffee brewing automatically in the morning.

In the realm of personal finance, smart home devices can contribute to energy savings, which translates to lower utility bills. Smart thermostats, for example, learn user habits and adjust heating and cooling accordingly, optimizing energy consumption without sacrificing comfort. Similarly, smart plugs and energy monitors can track the energy usage of individual devices, allowing homeowners to identify areas where they can cut costs. By employing these devices, users not only save money but also contribute to more sustainable living by reducing their overall carbon footprint.

For those interested in education, smart home devices can serve as valuable learning tools. Devices like smart displays can provide interactive lessons, tutorials, and resources tailored to users' interests. For children, platforms like Alexa can offer educational games and quizzes, making learning fun and engaging. Furthermore, these devices can facilitate learning in other languages or subjects through various apps and skills, turning everyday interactions into opportunities for growth and knowledge acquisition.

Finally, smart home devices are making significant strides in enhancing the shopping experience. With smart speakers and connected devices, users can receive personalized recommendations based on their purchasing history and preferences. Voice shopping has become increasingly popular, allowing users to order products hands-free. Additionally, smart home devices can track inventory and send alerts when supplies are running low, ensuring that users never run out of essential items. By integrating AI into shopping, these devices not only simplify the purchasing process but also help users discover deals that align with their needs and preferences.

AI in Communication

AI in Communication is reshaping the way we interact in our daily lives, making conversations more efficient and tailored to our needs. From chatbots that assist with customer service to virtual assistants that help manage our schedules, AI technologies are enhancing personal and professional communication. These tools can analyze language patterns, understand context, and respond with relevant information, allowing for smoother interactions. As a result, individuals can save time and reduce the frustration often associated with traditional communication methods.

One significant application of AI in communication is through language translation services. Tools such as Google Translate utilize machine learning algorithms to provide real-time translations, enabling people from different linguistic backgrounds to communicate effortlessly. This capability not only fosters better understanding among individuals but also opens up new opportunities for collaboration and networking across the globe. With such tools, users can engage in conversations, read content, and participate in discussions without the barrier of language proficiency.

AI is also enhancing communication in the realm of social media. Platforms are increasingly using algorithms to curate content and engage users based on their interests and preferences. This means that individuals can receive personalized updates, recommendations, and advertisements, making their online experience more relevant and enjoyable. Additionally, AI-driven analytics can help users understand their audience better, enabling businesses and content creators to tailor their messages for maximum impact. By analyzing engagement metrics, they can refine their strategies and enhance their communication effectiveness.

In the workplace, AI is transforming how teams collaborate and share information. Tools like Slack and Microsoft Teams incorporate AI features that facilitate communication by summarizing messages, scheduling meetings, and even providing insights based on previous conversations. These advancements enable teams to work more cohesively and productively, as important information is readily accessible, and communication flows more smoothly. As remote and hybrid work environments become increasingly common, such AI tools are crucial in maintaining clear and effective communication among team members.

Finally, AI is making significant strides in personal communication as well. Virtual assistants like Siri and Alexa can manage tasks, set reminders, and even engage in casual conversation. These technologies offer a hands-free way to communicate, allowing individuals to multitask while keeping their lives organized. As AI continues to evolve, we can expect even more sophisticated communication tools that not only assist with daily tasks but also enhance our ability to connect with others, fostering deeper relationships in both personal and professional contexts.

Chapter 3: AI for Time Management

Scheduling and Calendar Tools

In today's fast-paced world, effective scheduling and calendar tools are essential for managing time efficiently. Artificial intelligence has significantly transformed how we organize our lives, making it easier to prioritize tasks, plan events, and allocate time effectively. AI-driven calendar applications can analyze your habits and preferences, suggesting optimal times for meetings or reminders for important deadlines. By integrating with other applications, these tools streamline your daily activities, ensuring that you stay on top of both personal and professional commitments.

One of the most valuable features of AI scheduling tools is their ability to learn from user behavior. By observing how you manage your time, these applications can provide personalized suggestions that align with your work style. For instance, if you often schedule meetings in the morning, an AI tool can automate the process, proposing suitable time slots based on your availability. This not only saves time but also reduces the mental load associated with planning, allowing users to focus on more critical tasks.

In the realm of personal finance, AI can enhance scheduling by reminding users of upcoming bills or payment deadlines. By integrating financial calendars with budgeting tools, individuals can maintain oversight of their expenses while ensuring that they are meeting financial obligations on time. This proactive approach to financial management can significantly reduce stress and help users avoid late fees or missed payments, ultimately leading to better financial health.

AI tools also play a crucial role in educational settings by helping students manage their study schedules. By analyzing workload and deadlines, these tools can recommend study times and breaks, optimizing learning experiences. For instance, a student could receive reminders about upcoming exams or deadlines for assignments, along with suggestions for study blocks tailored to their preferences. This personalized approach can enhance productivity and improve learning outcomes, making education more accessible and less overwhelming.

Travel planning is another area where AI scheduling tools shine, simplifying the often complex process of organizing itineraries. AI-driven applications can automatically generate travel schedules, taking into account flight times, accommodation check-ins, and activity bookings. By providing users with a clear and organized travel plan, these tools reduce the potential for confusion and missed connections. Additionally, they can offer personalized recommendations based on user preferences, ensuring that every trip is tailored to individual tastes, making travel more enjoyable and efficient.

Task Management Applications

Task management applications have transformed the way individuals and te

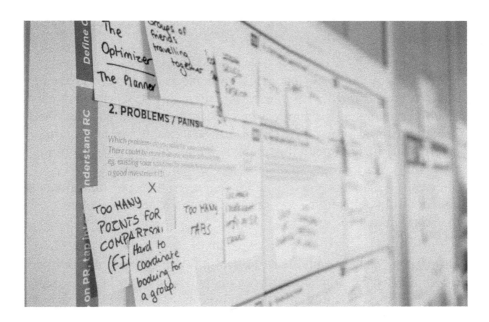

ams organize their activities and responsibilities. These tools utilize artificial intelligence to streamline processes, enhance productivity, and simplify the management of daily tasks. By integrating AI features such as smart scheduling, priority setting, and automated reminders, users can better allocate their time and resources, ensuring that important tasks are completed efficiently. For beginners, exploring these applications can significantly improve time management and overall productivity, making it easier to balance personal and professional commitments.

One of the key benefits of task management applications is their ability to adapt to individual user preferences and habits. AI algorithms analyze user behavior to provide personalized recommendations on task prioritization and scheduling. This adaptability means that beginners can receive tailored advice on how to structure their day, identifying which tasks require immediate attention and which can be deferred. By leveraging AI, these applications can help users avoid the common pitfalls of procrastination and overwhelm, making it easier to focus on what truly matters.

In the realm of personal finance, task management applications can also play a crucial role. By integrating budgeting tools and reminders for bill payments, these applications assist users in maintaining their financial responsibilities. AI-driven insights can highlight spending patterns, suggest budget adjustments, and notify users of upcoming payments, ensuring that financial management is seamless and efficient. This integration of task management with personal finance tools not only helps users stay organized but also fosters better financial habits over time.

For learners, task management applications can enhance educational experiences by helping students organize their study schedules and assignments. AI features can suggest optimal study times, track progress on projects, and even recommend resources based on the subjects being studied. This proactive approach to learning allows students to manage their academic workload effectively, leading to improved outcomes and a greater understanding of their subjects. By incorporating AI into their study routines, learners can maximize their educational potential and develop essential skills for lifelong success.

In creative fields, task management applications can aid artists, writers, and musicians by organizing projects and deadlines. AI tools can assist in brainstorming ideas, managing collaborative efforts, and tracking inspiration sources. By streamlining the creative process, these applications help users maintain focus and overcome creative blocks. Integrating AI into task management not only facilitates the organization of creative endeavors but also nurtures innovation, allowing individuals to explore and express their creativity without the constraints of chaos or disorganization.

Automation for Efficiency

In today's fast-paced world, the integration of artificial intelligence into everyday tasks has become a game-changer for enhancing efficiency. Automation allows individuals to streamline various processes, freeing up valuable time and resources. From managing schedules to automating mundane financial tasks, AI tools can help people maximize their productivity. By understanding how to leverage these technologies, anyone can transform their daily routines and achieve more with less effort.

One of the most significant advantages of AI-driven automation is its application in time management. Tools like smart calendars and scheduling assistants can analyze your preferences and suggest optimal times for meetings or appointments. For instance, AI can help in identifying gaps in your schedule and proposing the best times for both work and leisure activities. This not only aids in better organization but also reduces the cognitive load associated with planning, allowing individuals to focus on more critical tasks.

In personal finance, automation can revolutionize budgeting and investment strategies. AI-powered applications can track spending patterns, categorize expenses, and provide personalized insights to help users stay on budget. Additionally, these tools can automate saving by setting aside funds based on user-defined goals. Investment apps can use AI algorithms to analyze market trends and suggest optimal investment strategies, making financial planning more accessible even for those who may not have extensive financial knowledge.

Education has also seen a significant impact from AI automation. Learning platforms equipped with AI can personalize educational experiences by adapting to the unique learning styles and paces of individual students. These systems can automate the grading process, provide instant feedback, and suggest additional resources tailored to the learner's needs. This level of personalization not only enhances comprehension but also encourages continuous engagement with the material, making learning more effective and enjoyable.

Creative pursuits are not left out of the automation revolution. AI tools in art, music, and content creation have become increasingly popular, allowing users to generate unique works with minimal effort. For example, AI can help create original music compositions, assist in writing articles, or even generate visual art. These tools empower individuals to explore their creativity without being hindered by technical skill limitations. By integrating AI into creative processes, users can focus on ideation and inspiration rather than getting bogged down by the mechanics of creation, ultimately enhancing their creative output.

Chapter 4: AI in Personal Finance

Budgeting Tools

Budgeting tools powered by artificial intelligence have transformed the way individuals manage their finances. These tools not only help users keep track of their spending habits but also provide personalized insights and recommendations, making budgeting more accessible and efficient. For beginners, the array of AI-driven budgeting applications can be overwhelming. However, understanding key features and functionalities can simplify the process and empower users to take control of their financial health.

One of the most valuable aspects of AI budgeting tools is their ability to analyze spending patterns. By connecting with bank accounts and credit cards, these applications can categorize transactions automatically, highlighting areas where users may be overspending. This feature allows individuals to see a clear picture of their finances, making it easier to create a budget that aligns with their financial goals. Additionally, many tools offer visualizations, such as graphs and charts, which can further enhance understanding and engagement with personal finance.

AI budgeting tools also excel in providing tailored advice and reminders. For instance, some applications utilize machine learning algorithms to forecast future spending based on historical data, helping users anticipate their financial needs. Notifications can alert users when they are approaching budget limits or when bills are due, reducing the likelihood of late payments and associated fees. This proactive approach to financial management encourages discipline and fosters better spending habits.

Moreover, many AI-driven budgeting tools come equipped with features that encourage saving and investment. By analyzing income and expenses, these applications can suggest optimal savings strategies and investment opportunities tailored to individual risk preferences and financial goals. Users can set savings targets, and the AI will help track progress, making it easier to stay motivated and on track. This holistic approach to financial management can significantly enhance the overall user experience.

Finally, the integration of AI in budgeting tools extends to personalized recommendations, which can enhance shopping experiences and even travel planning. By learning about a user's preferences and spending behaviors, these applications can suggest deals, discounts, and budgeting strategies that align with personal interests. This not only saves money but also time, as users receive curated options that suit their needs. In this way, AI budgeting tools not only facilitate effective financial management but also enrich daily life through enhanced decision-making capabilities.

Investment Apps

Investment apps have emerged as powerful tools for individuals looking to manage their finances and grow their wealth through smart investing. These applications leverage artificial intelligence to analyze market trends, assess risks, and provide personalized investment recommendations tailored to the user's financial goals and risk tolerance. By simplifying complex financial data and offering user-friendly interfaces, investment apps make it easier for novices and experienced investors alike to navigate the world of stocks, bonds, and other investment vehicles.

One of the key features of many investment apps is their use of AI algorithms to provide real-time insights and analytics. These algorithms can process vast amounts of data, identifying patterns and trends that may not be immediately obvious to human investors. For example, an app might analyze historical stock performance, current market conditions, and even social media sentiment to give users a comprehensive view of potential investment opportunities. This level of analysis can empower users to make informed decisions, rather than relying solely on gut feelings or outdated advice.

Investment apps also often include educational tools designed to help users enhance their financial literacy. Many apps provide tutorials, articles, and interactive tools that explain the principles of investing, the various types of assets, and strategies for building a diversified portfolio. By integrating these educational resources directly into the app, users can learn at their own pace while actively managing their investments, making the process of investing less intimidating and more accessible to everyone.

Moreover, the convenience of investment apps cannot be overstated. Users can monitor their portfolios, execute trades, and track performance all from their smartphones or tablets, allowing for greater flexibility and responsiveness to market changes. Many apps also offer automated features, such as robo-advisors, which manage investments on behalf of users based on pre-set parameters. This automation can save time and reduce the stress associated with manual trading, making investment management more efficient.

Finally, investment apps often integrate social features that encourage community engagement and sharing of insights among users. This aspect not only fosters a sense of belonging but also facilitates learning from peers who may have different experiences and investment strategies. By combining technology, education, and community, investment apps represent a modern approach to personal finance, making investing more approachable and effective for everyone, regardless of their financial background.

Financial Planning and Analysis

Financial planning and analysis are crucial components of personal finance management, and with the advent of artificial intelligence, these processes have become more accessible and efficient for everyone. AI tools can help individuals assess their financial situations, set realistic goals, and create actionable plans to achieve them. By analyzing spending patterns and income streams, AI-driven applications can provide insights into where money is being spent excessively and where savings can be made. This level of analysis enables users to make informed decisions about budgeting, thereby allowing for a more secure financial future.

AI's role in budgeting is particularly transformative. Traditional budgeting methods often require tedious manual calculations and constant adjustments. AI tools can automate many of these tasks, offering real-time updates and recommendations based on current financial behavior. For instance, users can connect their bank accounts to budgeting apps that utilize AI algorithms to categorize expenses, track spending habits, and suggest budget adjustments. This streamlining of the budgeting process not only saves time but also enhances accuracy, making it easier for individuals to stay on top of their financial goals.

Investment assistance is another area where AI shines in financial planning and analysis. Many people find investing intimidating due to the complexities involved in understanding markets and making informed decisions. AI-driven investment platforms can analyze vast amounts of market data and identify trends that may not be immediately obvious to the average investor. These platforms can offer personalized investment strategies based on individual risk tolerance and financial objectives, making investing more accessible for beginners. With AI, users can receive tailored recommendations that help maximize returns while minimizing risks.

Furthermore, AI can simplify the process of long-term financial planning by providing users with predictive analytics. These tools can forecast future income, expenses, and investment growth based on historical data and current market trends. This capability allows individuals to visualize their financial future and adjust their plans accordingly. For example, if an AI tool predicts a significant increase in expenses due to an upcoming life event, users can proactively make adjustments to their budgets and savings strategies to accommodate these changes. This foresight empowers individuals to take control of their financial destinies.

Finally, the integration of AI into financial planning extends beyond individual budgeting and investment strategies. It also facilitates better decision-making regarding larger financial goals, such as purchasing a home or planning for retirement. AI can analyze various financial scenarios and simulate outcomes based on different variables, helping users understand the implications of their choices. By providing comprehensive analysis and tailored advice, AI tools not only enhance personal finance management but also contribute to a more informed and financially literate society.

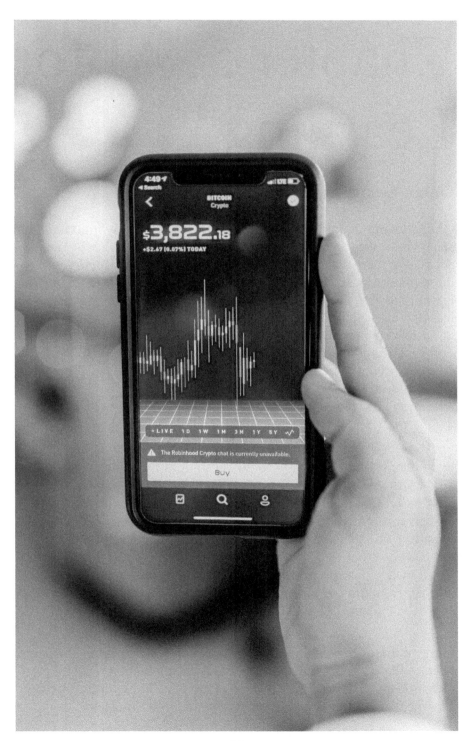

Chapter 5: AI for Learning

Online Learning Platforms

Online learning platforms have revolutionized the way individuals access education and training, making learning more flexible and accessible than ever before. With the rise of artificial intelligence, these platforms are becoming increasingly adept at personalizing the learning experience to meet individual needs. From adaptive learning algorithms that tailor course content to each learner's pace, to AI-driven analytics that provide insights into student performance, online learning platforms harness the power of AI to enhance educational outcomes. This transformation allows users to engage with material in a way that suits their unique learning styles, making education not only more effective but also more enjoyable.

For those looking to improve time management skills, online learning platforms offer a wealth of resources that leverage AI to help users prioritize tasks and manage their schedules more efficiently. Courses focusing on productivity tools often incorporate AI-driven applications that assist in setting reminders, automating repetitive tasks, and optimizing daily workflows. By integrating these tools into their learning journey, users can gain valuable skills that translate directly into their personal and professional lives, ultimately leading to better time management and a more organized approach to daily tasks.

In the realm of personal finance, online learning platforms provide courses that utilize AI to help users understand budgeting, investment strategies, and financial planning. These platforms can analyze user spending habits and suggest tailored financial strategies, enhancing learners' ability to make informed decisions. By engaging with educational content that combines AI insights with practical financial advice, users can develop a solid foundation in personal finance management, paving the way for smarter investments and healthier financial habits that last a lifetime.

Creativity is another area where online learning platforms shine, especially through courses that explore the intersection of AI and creative endeavors. Whether it's generating artwork, composing music, or creating content, AI tools available on these platforms allow learners to experiment and push the boundaries of their creativity. By utilizing AI-assisted design software or music composition tools, individuals can unlock new possibilities in their artistic expression, enabling them to produce unique works that may have been difficult to achieve without technological assistance.

Lastly, for those planning their travels, online learning platforms can simplify itinerary creation and booking processes through the use of AI. Courses that focus on travel planning often highlight AI tools that aggregate data from various sources, providing personalized recommendations for accommodations, activities, and transportation. By learning how to leverage these technologies, users can streamline their travel planning experience, ensuring they maximize their time and resources while exploring new destinations. This integration of AI into travel education not only enhances user experience but also empowers individuals to travel smarter and more efficiently.

AI-Powered Tutoring Services

AI-Powered Tutoring Services are transforming how students learn by providing personalized educational support tailored to individual needs. These services leverage advanced algorithms and machine learning to assess a student's strengths, weaknesses, and learning pace. Unlike traditional tutoring methods, AI-powered platforms can offer instant feedback and resources, making it easier for learners to grasp complex concepts in real-time. This adaptability not only enhances understanding but also fosters a more engaging educational experience.

One of the most significant advantages of AI tutoring services is their ability to provide customized learning experiences. These platforms analyze user data, such as previous performance and learning preferences, to create a personalized study plan. For example, if a student struggles with algebra, the AI can focus on specific problem areas, offering targeted exercises and resources that build foundational skills. This tailored approach ensures that students are not left behind and can progress at their own pace.

Furthermore, AI-powered tutoring services are available around the clock, providing learners with access to help whenever they need it. This flexibility is particularly beneficial for those juggling multiple responsibilities, such as work and family commitments. Students can engage with the platform at their convenience, ensuring that learning fits seamlessly into their daily lives. As a result, the barriers of time and location are significantly reduced, making education more accessible than ever before.

AI technology also facilitates the integration of various learning materials, including videos, interactive quizzes, and reading resources. This multimedia approach caters to different learning styles, whether visual, auditory, or kinesthetic. By employing a range of methods, AI tutoring services keep students engaged and motivated, making the learning process more enjoyable. As learners interact with diverse content, they can develop a deeper understanding of subjects and retain information more effectively.

In addition to enhancing individual learning experiences, AI-powered tutoring can support teachers and educational institutions. By analyzing performance data across a wide range of students, AI can identify trends and areas where the curriculum may need improvement. Educators can use these insights to refine their teaching strategies, ensuring that they address the needs of their students more effectively. As AI continues to evolve, its role in education will likely expand, paving the way for a future where personalized learning is the norm and every student has the opportunity to succeed.

Language Learning with AI

Language learning has evolved significantly with the advent of artificial intelligence, offering new opportunities for individuals to acquire new languages more efficiently and effectively. AI-powered tools are designed to cater to various learning styles and preferences, making it easier for users to engage with the content and practice their skills. From personalized lessons to instant feedback, AI has transformed the language learning landscape, enabling learners to immerse themselves in different languages at their own pace.

One of the most notable advantages of using AI in language learning is the ability to provide tailored instruction. AI algorithms analyze a learner's progress, strengths, and weaknesses, allowing them to create a customized curriculum that addresses their specific needs. This personalized approach helps learners focus on areas that require improvement, while also building on their existing knowledge. As a result, individuals can advance more quickly and confidently, making the process of learning a new language less daunting.

AI-driven language learning platforms often incorporate speech recognition technology, allowing users to practice their pronunciation and speaking skills in real-time. This feature not only helps learners develop their conversational abilities but also provides immediate feedback on their performance. By identifying pronunciation errors and offering corrective suggestions, AI tools enable users to refine their skills and become more proficient in their target language. This interactive aspect of learning greatly enhances engagement and encourages learners to practice more frequently.

Additionally, AI can facilitate immersive language experiences through chatbots and virtual conversation partners. These AI-powered tools simulate real-life conversations, allowing learners to practice their language skills in a supportive environment. By interacting with chatbots, users can experiment with vocabulary and grammar without the fear of making mistakes in front of a native speaker. This safe space fosters confidence and encourages learners to explore the nuances of the language, ultimately enhancing their communication skills.

As technology continues to advance, the integration of AI in language learning is expected to grow even more sophisticated. Future developments may include enhanced cultural context integration, allowing learners to not only grasp the language but also understand the cultural nuances that accompany it. Moreover, as AI becomes more accessible, a broader audience will benefit from these tools, making language learning a more inclusive and enriching experience for everyone. Embracing AI in language education can unlock doors to new opportunities and experiences, transforming how individuals connect with the world around them.

Chapter 6: Creative Uses of AI

AI in Art and Design

AI in art and design is revolutionizing the way creators approach their work, allowing for new levels of creativity and efficiency. Artists and designers are increasingly turning to AI tools to enhance their creative processes, whether it's through generating unique visuals, suggesting color palettes, or even composing music. These technologies can analyze vast datasets, offering insights and inspiration that might not have been easily accessible before. As a result, AI is becoming an essential partner in the creative fields, helping to break down barriers and expand the possibilities of what art and design can achieve.

One prominent application of AI in art is the use of generative algorithms. These systems can create original artwork by learning from existing pieces, mimicking styles, and generating new compositions. This approach allows artists to experiment with forms and styles that they may not have tried otherwise. For example, tools like DeepArt and Artbreeder enable users to create stunning visuals by blending different artistic styles or themes. This capability not only provides artists with new creative tools but also challenges traditional notions of authorship and originality in the art world.

In design, AI is streamlining workflows and enhancing productivity. Graphic designers can leverage AI tools for tasks such as automating repetitive design elements or optimizing layouts. Programs like Canva and Adobe Sensei incorporate AI features that help users make design decisions faster. For instance, AI can suggest design templates based on user preferences or analyze design trends to provide recommendations. This allows designers to focus more on the creative aspects of their work, ultimately leading to more innovative and polished results.

AI also plays a significant role in music composition and sound design. Tools like Amper Music and AIVA utilize machine learning algorithms to compose original music tracks, enabling creators to produce high-quality scores without needing extensive musical training. These platforms can analyze various musical styles and genres, offering users the ability to generate custom soundtracks for their projects. This democratization of music creation opens the door for anyone to explore their musical ideas, regardless of their background or expertise.

Finally, as AI continues to evolve, the collaborative potential between humans and machines in art and design is boundless. Artists are discovering that AI can act as a co-creator, providing fresh perspectives and ideas that enhance their own creative vision. By embracing these technologies, individuals can not only streamline their creative processes but also push the boundaries of what is possible in art and design. As we integrate AI into our daily lives, the fusion of technology and creativity will undoubtedly lead to exciting new forms of expression and innovation.

Music Composition and Production

Music composition and production have undergone a transformative shift with the advent of artificial intelligence. AI tools are now accessible to everyone, regardless of their musical background. These tools can assist both amateurs and professionals in creating, arranging, and producing music. From generating melodies to offering production advice, AI can serve as a collaborative partner in the creative process, making music composition more efficient and enjoyable.

One significant area where AI shines is in melody and chord progression generation. Various AI platforms allow users to input a few parameters, such as genre, mood, or tempo, and then generate original melodies or chord progressions. This capability can serve as an excellent starting point for songwriters experiencing writer's block or for those looking to experiment with new musical ideas. By leveraging these tools, users can save time and find inspiration that might not have emerged through traditional methods.

In addition to generating melodies, AI can significantly enhance the production process. AI-powered software can analyze existing tracks and suggest improvements in mixing and mastering. These tools can identify areas where the sound may be unbalanced and provide recommendations for adjustments. This not only helps improve the quality of the music but also allows producers to focus more on the creative aspects of their work rather than getting bogged down in technical details.

Furthermore, AI can aid in the personalization of music experiences. Platforms powered by AI can analyze a listener's preferences and suggest songs or playlists tailored to their tastes. This personalization extends to music streaming services that use algorithms to recommend new artists and tracks based on listening history. For musicians, understanding how AI curates music can help them reach their target audience more effectively by aligning their work with current trends and preferences.

Lastly, the integration of AI in music composition and production encourages collaboration across disciplines. Musicians can work alongside AI tools to create innovative sounds and styles that push the boundaries of traditional music genres. This collaboration not only democratizes music creation but also fosters a community where both AI and human creativity can thrive. As technology continues to evolve, the potential for AI in music will likely expand, offering even more opportunities for everyone to engage with and appreciate the art of music.

Content Creation and Writing

Content creation and writing have undergone a significant transformation with the advent of artificial intelligence. In the past, crafting engaging content required extensive knowledge and time. Today, AI tools can assist writers by generating ideas, suggesting topics, and even drafting entire articles. These innovations make it easier for anyone, regardless of their writing proficiency, to produce high-quality content. For beginners, leveraging AI in content creation can help overcome writer's block and inspire creativity, allowing individuals to focus on refining their ideas rather than getting stuck on the initial concept.

AI-powered writing assistants can analyze vast amounts of data to identify trending topics and relevant keywords, ensuring that the content resonates with target audiences. This capability is particularly beneficial for those managing blogs or social media accounts, as it allows for the creation of timely and engaging posts that attract attention. Furthermore, these tools can optimize content for search engines, enhancing visibility and reach. By integrating AI into their writing process, users can not only save time but also improve their chances of connecting with readers and driving engagement.

The application of AI in content creation extends beyond just text. Many tools can also assist in producing multimedia content, such as images and videos. For instance, AI can generate graphics or suggest layouts that complement written content, creating a more dynamic user experience. This integration of visual elements enhances storytelling and helps convey messages more effectively. For those looking to create comprehensive online content, AI provides the necessary resources to streamline both the writing and visual aspects of their projects.

Moreover, AI tools can facilitate collaboration among multiple content creators. Platforms that incorporate AI can help track contributions, suggest edits, and manage feedback in real-time. This collaborative environment fosters creativity and innovation, as team members can build upon each other's ideas more efficiently. For organizations or groups working on joint projects, utilizing AI for content creation can enhance productivity and ensure that the final product is cohesive and well-structured.

In summary, the intersection of AI and content creation offers a plethora of opportunities for writers, marketers, and creative individuals. By harnessing these advanced tools, users can enhance their writing process, produce engaging content, and effectively communicate their ideas. As AI continues to evolve, embracing these technologies will be essential for anyone looking to thrive in the digital landscape, allowing for greater creativity and efficiency in daily content creation endeavors.

Chapter 7: AI for Travel Planning

Itinerary Planning Tools

Itinerary planning tools powered by artificial intelligence are revolutionizing the way we organize our travels. These tools utilize advanced algorithms to analyze user preferences, past travel experiences, and real-time data, enabling travelers to create personalized travel itineraries with ease. Whether planning a weekend getaway or a month-long adventure, AI-driven tools can suggest optimal routes, recommend activities based on interests, and even help manage travel budgets. As a beginner, understanding how to leverage these technologies can transform the often tedious task of planning into an exciting preview of your upcoming journey.

AI itinerary planning tools can streamline the process of selecting destinations and activities. By aggregating data from various sources, these platforms can provide tailored recommendations based on your interests, travel history, and even social media activity. For instance, if you enjoy outdoor activities, an AI tool might suggest hiking trails, national parks, or adventure sports in your chosen destination. This personalized approach not only saves time but also enhances the overall travel experience by ensuring that the itinerary resonates with your preferences.

Additionally, AI tools can optimize travel logistics, which is a crucial aspect of any itinerary. By analyzing flight options, accommodation prices, and local transportation methods, these tools can suggest the most efficient travel plans. They can alert you to price drops on flights or accommodations, helping you secure the best deals available. Furthermore, some AI planners can integrate real-time updates, allowing you to adjust your itinerary based on unexpected changes such as flight delays or weather conditions. This dynamic flexibility is especially beneficial for today's travelers, who seek both efficiency and adaptability.

Incorporating AI into your travel planning not only enhances the quality of your experiences but also contributes to effective time management. With the ability to quickly generate and modify itineraries, these tools free up valuable time that can be redirected toward other important aspects of travel preparation, such as packing or arranging necessary documents. This efficiency is particularly beneficial for busy individuals who juggle work and personal commitments. By automating the planning process, AI allows them to focus on enjoying their travels rather than getting bogged down in logistical details.

Finally, as technology continues to evolve, the integration of AI into travel planning is likely to expand even further. Future developments may include more advanced predictive analytics that can anticipate traveler needs or preferences based on emerging trends. As these tools become more sophisticated, they will not only simplify the itinerary planning process but also enrich the travel experience itself. By embracing these advancements, users can stay ahead of the curve, ensuring that their travels are not only well-planned but also deeply rewarding.

Booking Assistance

Booking assistance through AI has transformed the way we plan our travel and manage our daily activities. With an array of advanced tools available, individuals can streamline the booking process for flights, accommodations, and entertainment, significantly reducing the time and effort traditionally required. AI algorithms analyze vast amounts of data to provide personalized recommendations based on user preferences, past behaviors, and current trends. This capability not only enhances the user experience but also ensures that travelers receive the best possible options tailored to their unique needs.

AI-powered travel platforms offer intuitive interfaces that allow users to search for flights, hotels, and rental cars efficiently. By inputting their travel dates and preferred destinations, users can receive instant suggestions that compare prices across multiple providers. These platforms often incorporate machine learning to adapt over time, becoming more accurate in predicting user preferences. As a result, travelers can find deals that may not be visible through conventional search methods, making the process both cost-effective and user-friendly.

In addition to finding the best deals, AI can assist with itinerary management. Tools equipped with AI capabilities can create comprehensive itineraries that include not only travel and accommodation details but also suggestions for activities and dining options. This is particularly useful for those who may feel overwhelmed by the sheer volume of choices available. By curating these recommendations based on user interests and local insights, AI helps ensure that travelers make the most of their trips while minimizing the stress of planning.

Furthermore, AI-driven booking assistants can provide real-time updates and alerts regarding travel changes, such as flight delays or gate changes. This proactive approach allows travelers to adjust their plans accordingly, eliminating potential disruptions. Through mobile applications or smart devices, users can receive notifications that keep them informed throughout their journey. This feature enhances safety and convenience, allowing individuals to focus on enjoying their travel experiences rather than worrying about logistics.

As AI continues to advance, its role in booking assistance will likely expand, incorporating even more sophisticated features such as virtual travel agents or chatbots for instant communication. These innovations promise to further simplify the booking process and enhance user experience. For everyday users, embracing AI in travel planning not only saves time and effort but also opens up a world of possibilities, making travel more accessible and enjoyable than ever before.

Travel Recommendations

Traveling can be an exhilarating experience, but planning a trip often involves considerable time and effort. Artificial intelligence can simplify this process, making travel planning more efficient and enjoyable. From generating personalized itineraries to providing real-time updates on flights and accommodations, AI tools can enhance your travel experience. For anyone looking to travel smarter, leveraging AI can lead to more organized trips, reduced stress, and even cost savings.

When planning a trip, AI-powered platforms such as travel apps and websites can analyze your preferences and suggest destinations that align with your interests. By inputting criteria such as budget, preferred activities, and travel dates, these tools can curate tailored itineraries that save time and enhance your overall travel experience. Additionally, AI can track trends and provide insights into popular destinations, helping you discover hidden gems you might not have considered otherwise.

Booking accommodations and transportation can be one of the most tedious parts of travel planning. AI-driven tools simplify this process by comparing prices across various platforms, allowing you to find the best deals without extensive research. Services like chatbots can assist in the booking process, answering questions in real time and ensuring that your reservations are completed efficiently. These intelligent systems eliminate the guesswork often associated with travel arrangements, allowing you to focus on the excitement of your upcoming adventure.

During your travels, AI can continue to play a pivotal role. Mobile applications equipped with AI capabilities can provide real-time updates on flight statuses, weather conditions, and traffic patterns. This ensures that you stay informed and can adjust your plans on the fly, whether you need to find an alternative route or locate a nearby restaurant. Furthermore, language translation apps powered by AI can facilitate communication in foreign countries, breaking down barriers and enhancing your interactions with locals.

Finally, upon returning home, AI can assist in preserving your travel memories. With tools that can help organize photos, create digital albums, or even compile travel blogs, AI offers creative outlets to document your experiences. The integration of AI in travel not only streamlines the planning and execution of trips but also enriches the overall journey, making it more memorable and enjoyable. By embracing these technologies, travelers can ensure they maximize their adventures while minimizing stress and logistical burdens.

Chapter 8: AI in Shopping

Personalized Shopping Experiences

Personalized shopping experiences have transformed the way consumers interact with retail, both online and in physical stores. By leveraging artificial intelligence, retailers can analyze vast amounts of data from customer behavior, preferences, and purchase history to tailor experiences that are uniquely suited to each individual. This level of personalization goes beyond simple recommendations; it creates a shopping environment where customers feel understood, valued, and catered to, making the process more enjoyable and efficient.

AI algorithms track user interactions with products, enabling retailers to provide personalized product suggestions based on previous purchases and browsing history. For instance, if a customer frequently buys athletic wear, AI can highlight new arrivals in that category or suggest complementary products like footwear or fitness accessories. This not only streamlines the shopping process but also enhances the likelihood of additional purchases, benefiting both the consumer and the retailer. The more data AI collects, the better it becomes at predicting what products a shopper may want next, creating a seamless experience tailored to individual tastes.

Moreover, personalized shopping experiences can extend to pricing and promotions. Through AI analysis, retailers can identify the optimal discount or promotional offer for each customer, based on their shopping behavior and sensitivity to pricing. For example, a customer who frequently makes impulse buys might receive a limited-time offer on items they have shown interest in, encouraging quicker decisions and enhancing sales. This strategy allows retailers to foster customer loyalty while optimizing their pricing strategies, leading to a win-win scenario.

In addition to online platforms, AI is also making strides in brick-and-mortar stores. With the integration of mobile apps and in-store technology, customers can receive personalized recommendations while shopping in real-time. For instance, by using location-based services, a shopper's app can notify them of relevant promotions or suggest items based on their preferences as they navigate the store aisles. This not only enhances the shopping experience but also helps retailers better manage inventory and understand consumer trends.

As consumers become increasingly accustomed to personalized shopping experiences, the role of AI in this domain will continue to evolve. The future may see even more sophisticated applications of AI, such as virtual shopping assistants or chatbots that can answer questions and provide tailored recommendations. By embracing these technologies, consumers can maximize their shopping efficiency, save time, and enjoy a more satisfying retail experience that caters to their unique needs and preferences.

Price Comparison and Deal Finding

Price comparison and deal finding have become significantly easier with the integration of artificial intelligence into our daily lives. AI tools can help consumers access real-time data on product prices across various platforms, allowing for informed purchasing decisions. By analyzing vast datasets, these AI applications can identify the best deals available, factoring in discounts, seasonal sales, and promotional offers. This capability not only saves time but also ensures that users get the most value for their money.

One of the most popular applications of AI in this domain is the use of price comparison websites and apps. These platforms utilize algorithms to scan multiple retailers simultaneously, presenting users with a comprehensive overview of prices for specific products. By simply inputting the desired item, consumers can quickly see where to buy it at the lowest price. Additionally, many of these tools can alert users when prices drop or when a product goes on sale, making it easier to purchase items at the right moment.

AI-driven chatbots and virtual assistants also play a crucial role in price comparison and deal finding. These intelligent systems can engage with users to understand their preferences and needs, providing personalized recommendations based on past purchases and browsing behavior. For instance, if a user frequently shops for electronics, the AI can prioritize deals and products in that category, ensuring a tailored shopping experience. This personalization enhances user satisfaction and can lead to significant savings over time.

In the realm of personal finance, AI tools can assist users in budgeting by analyzing spending patterns and identifying areas where they can save money. By integrating deal finding capabilities, these applications can suggest alternative products or services that offer similar benefits at a lower cost. This not only helps users manage their finances more effectively but also encourages smarter shopping habits. Over time, users can build a more sustainable financial plan that accommodates their lifestyle while maximizing savings.

As AI continues to evolve, the future of price comparison and deal finding looks promising. Advancements in machine learning and data analysis may lead to even more sophisticated tools that can predict price trends, suggest optimal purchasing times, and cater to individual consumer preferences with remarkable accuracy. By embracing these AI technologies, consumers can enhance their shopping experiences, making informed decisions that contribute to better financial health and overall satisfaction.

Virtual Try-Ons and Product Recommendations

Virtual try-ons and product recommendations represent a significant advancement in the way consumers interact with brands and products. This technology leverages artificial intelligence to create immersive shopping experiences that enhance decision-making. With virtual try-ons, shoppers can visualize how clothes, accessories, or cosmetics will look on them without physically trying them on. This not only saves time but also reduces the need for returns, as customers can make more informed purchasing decisions based on realistic simulations.

AI algorithms analyze a user's preferences, past purchases, and even body dimensions to curate personalized product recommendations. When shopping online, consumers are often overwhelmed by countless options. AI tools sift through this vast array of products to highlight the ones that best match individual tastes and needs. This personalization not only simplifies the shopping process but also fosters a deeper connection between consumers and brands, as customers feel understood and valued.

In the realm of fashion, virtual try-on technology is particularly transformative. By using augmented reality, consumers can see how clothes fit and look on their own bodies through their smartphones or computers. Brands that adopt this technology can enhance customer satisfaction by allowing users to experiment with styles and colors, leading to more confident purchases. This innovative approach not only boosts sales but also builds brand loyalty as customers appreciate the interactive experience.

The integration of AI in product recommendations extends beyond just fashion. In personal finance, for example, AI-driven platforms can suggest financial products tailored to individual spending habits and investment goals. Similarly, educational tools utilize AI to recommend learning materials that align with a student's interests and proficiency levels, making the learning process more engaging and effective. This level of customization is what sets AI apart from traditional methods, as it adapts to the unique characteristics of each user.

As consumers become increasingly accustomed to these personalized experiences, the demand for AI-driven solutions will likely grow. For travelers, AI can recommend destinations based on previous trips and preferences, while in creative domains, it can suggest tools and resources that align with personal artistic styles. The convenience and efficiency provided by AI in everyday scenarios, such as shopping or travel planning, not only enhance user experiences but also open up new possibilities for how we approach daily tasks and decisions.

Chapter 9: Ethical Considerations in AI

Privacy and Data Security

Privacy and data security have become paramount concerns in the age of artificial intelligence. As AI applications continue to permeate various aspects of daily life, from personal finance management to travel planning, users must be aware of how their data is collected, stored, and utilized. Understanding the implications of data privacy is essential for making informed choices about which AI tools to adopt. This awareness ensures that your sensitive information—ranging from financial details to personal preferences—is adequately protected against unauthorized access and misuse.

When utilizing AI in time management, users often input personal schedules and tasks into various applications. These tools analyze data to optimize productivity, but it is crucial to evaluate their privacy policies. Some applications may share user data with third parties or utilize it for targeted advertising. To safeguard your information, look for tools that offer end-to-end encryption and transparent privacy practices. Researching reviews and recommendations can also help identify trustworthy applications that prioritize user data security.

In the realm of personal finance, AI tools play an increasingly significant role in budgeting and investment assistance. While these applications can provide valuable insights and recommendations, they often require access to sensitive financial information. Users should ensure that any financial AI tool they choose employs robust security measures, such as two-factor authentication and secure data storage. Additionally, understanding how these tools handle data can help users maintain control over their financial information, ensuring that it is used solely for its intended purpose.

Education is another area where AI is making strides, providing tailored learning experiences and resources. However, educational tools often collect data on user progress and preferences. Users must be vigilant about the extent of data collection and how it is used. Opt for platforms that prioritize student privacy and offer features that allow users to control their data. By selecting educational AI tools with strong privacy protections, learners can enjoy personalized experiences without compromising their personal information.

Finally, as AI transforms shopping experiences through personalized recommendations, consumers should be aware of how their shopping habits and preferences are tracked. Many retail AI systems gather extensive data to enhance user experience, but this can lead to potential privacy breaches if not handled properly. Always read the privacy policies of shopping applications and utilize those that provide clear commitments to data security. By being proactive about privacy and data security, users can confidently embrace the benefits of AI in their daily lives while minimizing risks associated with data exposure.

Bias in AI Systems

Bias in AI systems is an increasingly critical issue that affects various aspects of daily life, from the tools we use for time management to personalized shopping experiences. At its core, bias refers to the systematic favoritism toward certain groups or outcomes based on flawed data or unexamined assumptions. This can lead to significant discrepancies in how AI applications perform across different demographics, thereby influencing decision-making processes in personal finance, education, and even creative endeavors. As individuals integrate AI into their daily routines, understanding the sources and implications of bias becomes essential for making informed choices.

One common source of bias in AI arises from the data used to train these systems. If the data reflects historical inequalities or lacks diversity, the AI is likely to perpetuate those biases. For instance, an AI tool designed to assist with budgeting and investment may be trained on data that predominantly represents specific income levels or demographic groups. Consequently, users from underrepresented backgrounds might receive less relevant or even harmful financial advice, limiting their opportunities for success. Recognizing this potential pitfall is crucial for anyone relying on AI for personal finance management.

In the realm of education, biased AI systems can hinder students' learning experiences. Educational tools that leverage AI for personalized learning paths may inadvertently favor certain learning styles or backgrounds over others. This could result in an unequal educational experience, where some students receive more tailored support while others are overlooked. As learners increasingly turn to AI-driven resources, it is vital to ensure that these tools are designed with equity in mind, promoting inclusivity and accessibility for all students.

Creative uses of AI, such as generating art or music, also face challenges related to bias. The algorithms that power these creative tools often draw from existing works, which may predominantly reflect specific cultural viewpoints. As a result, the outputs can lack diversity and fail to represent a broader spectrum of human experience. Understanding how bias can shape creative AI outputs encourages users to seek out diverse tools and platforms that foster a richer artistic expression.

Lastly, when it comes to travel planning and shopping, biased AI can lead to skewed recommendations that do not cater to a diverse range of preferences. For example, an AI travel planner might prioritize destinations popular among a specific demographic, leaving out valuable experiences for others. Similarly, shopping algorithms may push products that align with narrow consumer profiles, potentially overlooking unique needs and tastes. By being aware of these biases, individuals can make more conscious decisions about the AI systems they choose to engage with, ensuring they receive personalized and relevant recommendations that truly reflect their interests and values.

The Future of AI and Society

The future of artificial intelligence (AI) in society holds significant promise and potential challenges across various aspects of daily life. As AI technologies continue to advance, they are becoming increasingly integrated into our everyday activities, enhancing our capabilities in ways that were once thought to be the realm of science fiction. From personal assistants that help manage our schedules to sophisticated algorithms that optimize our finances, AI is reshaping how we interact with the world. This transformation is not merely about efficiency; it is about reimagining our relationship with technology and the possibilities it offers.

In the realm of time management, AI tools are set to become indispensable. Applications that analyze our habits, preferences, and schedules will enable users to streamline their tasks and prioritize effectively. For instance, AI-driven calendars can automatically suggest optimal meeting times, while task management apps can adapt to changing priorities. This level of personalization allows individuals to focus on what truly matters, reducing stress and enhancing productivity. As these tools evolve, they will likely incorporate more advanced features, such as predictive analytics, to foresee potential scheduling conflicts before they arise.

Personal finance is another area where AI will play a crucial role in shaping the future. Budgeting apps powered by AI can analyze spending patterns, suggest savings strategies, and even provide tailored investment advice based on individual financial goals. As AI continues to learn from user behavior, its recommendations will become increasingly accurate and relevant. This democratization of financial advice means that anyone can access tools that were previously available only to those with specialized knowledge, empowering individuals to take control of their financial futures.

Education is also set to undergo a transformation due to AI advancements. Learning platforms that utilize AI can offer personalized educational experiences by adapting to each student's pace and learning style. These tools can identify areas where a learner struggles and provide additional resources or exercises to reinforce understanding. As AI continues to advance, it will facilitate a more inclusive learning environment, making education accessible to a broader range of learners, including those with diverse needs and backgrounds.

In creative fields, AI is breaking new ground by assisting artists, musicians, and writers in their creative processes. Tools that generate music, create visual art, or assist in writing are becoming more sophisticated, allowing creators to explore new styles and ideas. This collaboration between humans and AI not only enhances the creative process but also raises questions about authorship and originality. As AI becomes a more common collaborator in creative endeavors, society will need to navigate the implications of these partnerships, embracing the innovations they bring while considering the ethical dimensions of their use.

Chapter 10: Getting Started with AI

Choosing the Right Tools

Choosing the right tools for integrating artificial intelligence into your daily life can significantly enhance your productivity and decision-making processes. With an array of options available, it's essential to evaluate each tool's features, usability, and relevance to your specific needs. In the realm of time management, for instance, AI-powered applications can help streamline tasks by automating reminders, scheduling meetings, and prioritizing your to-do list. Tools like Todoist or Trello utilize AI to suggest optimal task arrangements and deadlines, ensuring you stay organized and focused throughout your day.

In personal finance, selecting the appropriate AI tools can transform how you manage your budget and investments. Applications such as Mint or Personal Capital leverage artificial intelligence to analyze your spending habits, suggest savings strategies, and even provide investment advice tailored to your financial goals. These tools not only simplify budgeting but also help you make informed decisions about where to allocate your resources, maximizing your returns over time. By carefully assessing these options, you can choose a platform that aligns with your financial aspirations and offers user-friendly features.

For learners and educators alike, AI-powered educational tools can significantly enhance the learning experience. Platforms like Duolingo or Khan Academy employ AI to personalize learning paths, adapting to the individual pace and style of each user. By selecting tools that cater to your specific educational needs, whether language learning or skill development, you can make your study time more efficient and enjoyable. The right educational resources can foster a deeper understanding of subjects and encourage continuous growth, making learning a more engaging endeavor.

Creative individuals can also benefit from AI tools designed for art, music, and content creation. Applications like Canva for graphic design or Amper Music for music composition utilize AI to simplify the creative process, allowing users to produce high-quality work without extensive technical skills. By exploring various options, you can find tools that not only inspire creativity but also streamline the production process, enabling you to bring your ideas to life more efficiently. Choosing the right creative tools can enhance your projects and encourage experimentation in your artistic pursuits.

When it comes to travel planning, AI can significantly reduce the stress associated with organizing itineraries and bookings. Tools like Google Travel and Hopper use AI algorithms to analyze flight and hotel prices, providing users with personalized recommendations based on preferences and past behavior. By utilizing these tools, travelers can save time and money while ensuring their trips are tailored to their needs. Understanding the capabilities of these travel tools allows you to make informed choices and plan memorable journeys with ease. Ultimately, the right AI tools can transform various aspects of your daily life, making tasks more manageable and enjoyable.

Tips for Integration into Daily Life

To effectively integrate artificial intelligence into your daily life, start by identifying specific areas where AI can enhance your productivity and overall experience. Consider your routine tasks, such as scheduling, budgeting, or learning new skills. By pinpointing these areas, you can focus on the most relevant tools and applications that align with your needs. For instance, if time management is a priority, explore AI-driven calendar apps that automate scheduling and provide reminders, streamlining your daily activities.

Incorporating AI into personal finance can greatly simplify budgeting and investment decisions. Utilize AI-powered budgeting apps that analyze your spending habits and suggest tailored savings plans. These tools can help you make informed financial choices by providing insights into your financial health. Additionally, consider leveraging AI investment platforms that offer personalized portfolio recommendations based on your risk tolerance and financial goals, making investment more accessible and efficient.

For those looking to enhance their learning experiences, AI offers a plethora of educational tools that can adapt to individual learning styles. Platforms that utilize AI can provide personalized learning paths, suggest resources based on your progress, and even assess your understanding through quizzes. Incorporating these tools into your study routine not only makes learning more engaging but also allows you to track your progress over time, ensuring a more effective educational journey.

Creative individuals can also benefit from AI by exploring its applications in art, music, and content creation. AI tools can assist in generating ideas, providing inspiration, or even creating pieces of art or music based on your preferences. By experimenting with these creative AI applications, you can enhance your artistic practice and discover new forms of expression. This integration not only fosters creativity but also encourages collaboration between human ingenuity and machine learning.

Lastly, AI can significantly enhance your travel planning and shopping experiences. Use AI-driven travel apps that analyze your preferences and suggest personalized itineraries, including accommodations and activities tailored to your interests. In shopping, AI can provide personalized recommendations based on your browsing and purchasing history, helping you discover deals that align with your tastes. By embracing these AI tools in your daily life, you can save time, reduce stress, and make more informed decisions, ultimately leading to a more efficient and enjoyable lifestyle.

Resources for Continued Learning

In the rapidly evolving landscape of artificial intelligence, continuous learning is essential for individuals seeking to harness the power of AI in their daily lives. Numerous resources are available that cater to different aspects of AI, from practical applications in personal finance to creative endeavors in art and music. For those new to AI, starting with beginner-friendly platforms and guides can establish a solid foundation. Websites such as Coursera and edX offer courses specifically designed to introduce AI concepts and practical applications, making it easy for anyone to learn at their own pace.

For individuals looking to integrate AI into time management and productivity, tools like Todoist and Trello are equipped with AI features that help prioritize tasks and optimize schedules. Blogs and podcasts focusing on productivity can provide insights into how AI tools can streamline daily routines. Online forums such as Reddit or specialized Facebook groups can also serve as valuable platforms for exchanging tips and experiences with other users, fostering a community of learners eager to share their strategies for maximizing efficiency using AI.

In the realm of personal finance, numerous apps utilize AI to assist with budgeting and investment management. Resources like NerdWallet and Investopedia offer articles and tutorials on these AI-driven tools. Additionally, webinars and online workshops can provide deeper insights into utilizing AI for financial planning. Engaging with financial influencers on platforms like YouTube or Instagram can also present practical tips on using AI to optimize savings and investment strategies, making complex concepts more accessible.

Educational tools powered by AI have transformed the way we learn, providing personalized experiences that cater to individual learning styles. Platforms like Khan Academy and Duolingo use AI algorithms to adapt content to the learner's pace, making education more engaging and effective. Supplementing these tools with online communities and study groups can enhance the learning experience. Participating in discussions on platforms such as Discord or Slack can help learners exchange knowledge, thereby solidifying their understanding of AI applications in education.

Creative uses of AI are growing in popularity, offering tools that assist in generating art, music, and content. Resources like OpenAI's DALL-E for image generation and AIVA for music composition showcase how AI can augment creative processes. Aspiring creators can explore online tutorials on platforms like YouTube, which often provide step-by-step guides on using these tools effectively. Engaging with creative communities, whether through social media or dedicated forums, can inspire collaboration and innovation, allowing individuals to explore the limitless possibilities of AI in their artistic pursuits.